From Your Friends At **The MAILBOX®**

W9-ATX-388

JANUARY

A MONTH OF REPRODUCIBLES AT YOUR FINGERTIPS!

Kindergarten

Editors:
Ada Goren
Angie Kutzer

Writers:
Joe Appleton, Susan Bunyan, Susan DeRiso, Rhonda Dominguez,
Henry Fergus, Diane Gilliam, Lucia Kemp Henry, Kelli Plaxco

Art Coordinator:
Clevell Harris

Artists:
Jennifer Tipton Bennett, Pam Crane, Nick Greenwood,
Clevell Harris, Lucia Kemp Henry, Susan Hodnett,
Sheila Krill, Rob Mayworth, Kimberly Richard,
Rebecca Saunders, Barry Slate, Donna K. Teal

Cover Artist:
Jennifer Tipton Bennett

©1999 by THE EDUCATION CENTER, INC.
All rights reserved.
ISBN #1-56234-280-0

Manufactured in the United States

10 9 8 7 6 5 4 3 2 1

Table Of Contents

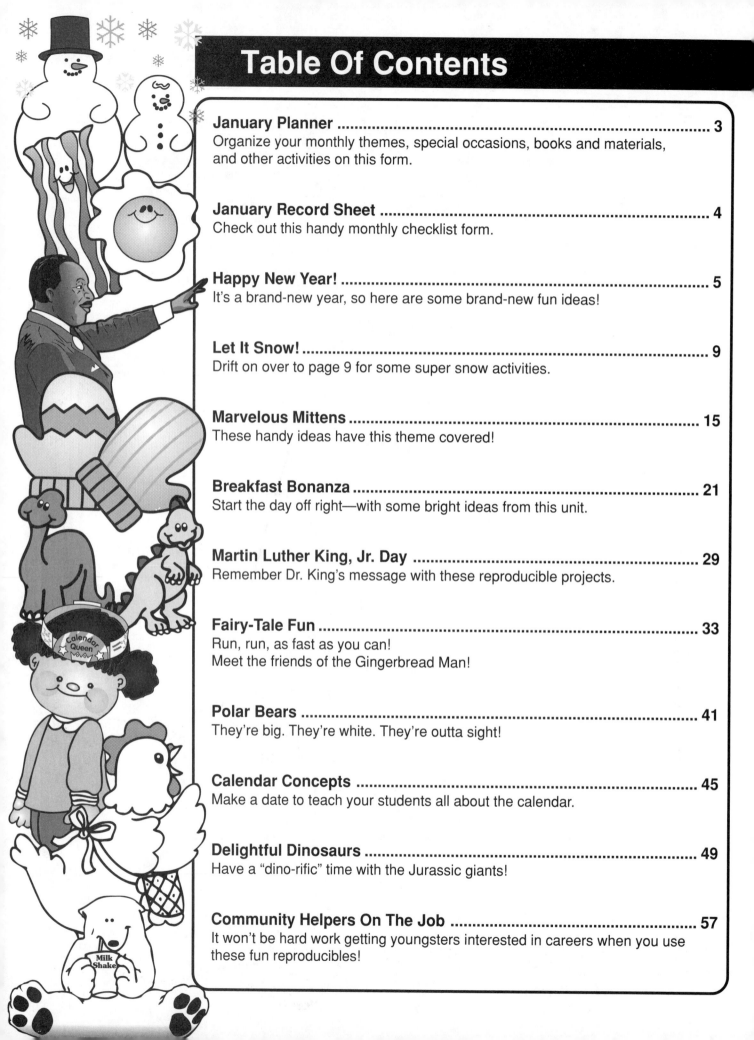

Materials To Collect:

JANUARY Classroom Themes:

Duties This Month:

Books To Check Out:

To Do:

MEETINGS:

Birthdays:

Special Dates:

JANUARY

©1999 The Education Center, Inc. • *January Monthly Reproducibles* • Kindergarten • TEC935

HAPPY NEW YEAR!

Give a cheer for a brand-new year *and* for these creative ideas to help you and your students celebrate!

New Year's Party In A Bag

Help youngsters prepare these celebration kits, complete with everything needed for a New Year's welcome. Use the completed kits at school, or send them home for family revelry. To begin, have each child complete the dot-to-dot design on a copy of page 6. Then invite her to color the finished picture and cut it out along the bold lines. Staple the picture to one side of a gallon-size zippered plastic bag. Then fill the bag with an uninflated balloon or two, a party horn or blower, and the projects made in "Whee!", "I Resolve To...," and "Countdown." There you have it—a party in a bag!

Whee!

No New Year's celebration would be complete without the appropriate decorations. Duplicate a class supply of the streamer pattern on page 7 onto white construction paper. Have each child use watercolor markers to decorate the entire page. Help him cut out the streamer, following the bold lines on both the outside and the inside of the spiral. Then have him cut the remaining scraps of paper into small pieces. Now you're ready with a streamer and confetti!

Countdown

Some of your youngsters may have seen the traditional ball-drop in Times Square on television. Help your youngsters make this countdown prop so they can practice their midnight math. Duplicate a class supply of page 8. To make one countdown prop, cut out the strips (including the dotted box) and glue them together as shown. Decorate the ball shape with glitter and let it dry. Color the countdown base; then cut it out and make two slits as indicated. Slide the strip into the top slit from back to front and then into the bottom slit from front to back. Position the glittery ball over the numeral 10 at the top; then pull the strip down and count off each number that shows in the opening until you reach the message "Happy New Year!"

I Resolve To...

Explain to your students that New Year's Day is a time when many people make *resolutions*—promises to themselves about new things they will do or ways they will act. Ask each of your youngsters to think about a resolution he could make for the coming year. Then duplicate a class supply of the resolution card on page 7. Have each child fill in the year and then write or dictate his resolution. Have him add an illustration, if desired.

5

Dot-To-Dot Bag Cover

Use with "New Year's Party In A Bag" on page 5.

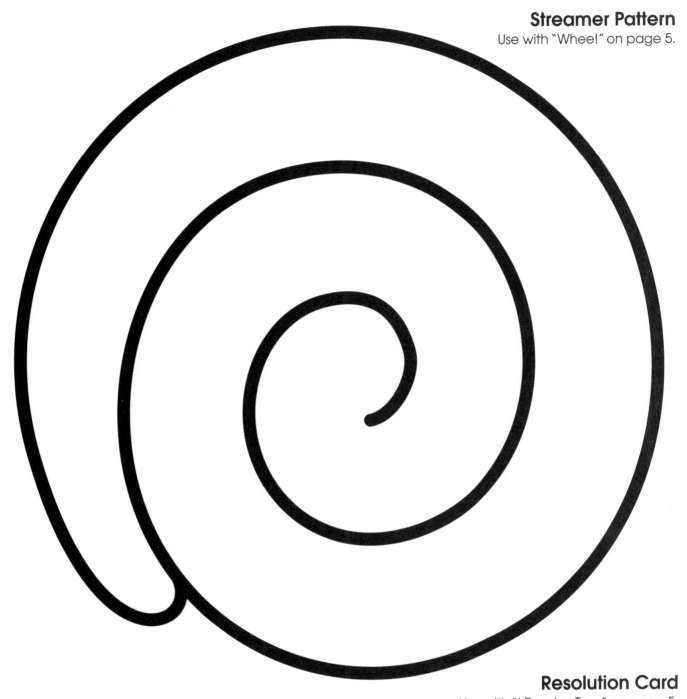

Resolution Card
Use with "I Resolve To…" on page 5.

In _____,

I resolve to _____

_____

_____.

Countdown Prop
Use with "Countdown" on page 5.

Let's Count Down

10
9
8
7
6
5
4
3
2
1

Happy
New
Year!

To A New Year!

Overlap and glue here.

Let It Snow!

Wishing for a flurry of cool reproducibles? Then plow into this collection of snowy ideas!

It's "Snow" Much Fun To Read!

When the weather outside is frightful, reading is *so* delightful! Encourage your little ones to curl up with a good book—or two or three—with a snowy reading incentive. Duplicate page 10 on white construction paper for each child. Have each child personalize his snowflake; then send home the patterns and ask each family to record six books read at home. Once a child has recorded six titles, invite him to use white or silver glitter to decorate the tips of his snowflake before cutting it out. Display the finished flakes around a door or on a bulletin board with a black or blue background.

Snowy Story Sequencing

After a reading of *The Snowy Day* by Ezra Jack Keats (Scholastic Inc.), challenge students to sequence the events in the story. To prepare, duplicate a class supply of page 11. Share the book with your students; then ask them to recall the things that Peter does in the snow. Reread the book so students can focus on the sequence of events. Then give each child a copy of page 11. Have him color the cards, cut them apart, and glue them in sequence on a 6" x 18" strip of construction paper.

Pattern-Block Snowflakes

Your little ones will have an avalanche of fun creating these pattern-block snowflakes! Provide each child with a supply of pattern blocks and a copy of page 12. Direct each student to place the corresponding pattern blocks on top of each pattern, then slide the blocks aside to color the spaces accordingly. Invite her to find a new combination of pattern blocks to complete the last snowflake on the page.

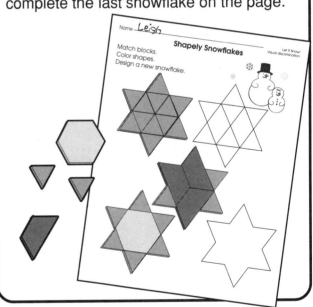

Snowy Skill Builders

For some frosty phonemic awareness, give each child a copy of page 13. Help students identify each picture at the bottom of the page. Then have each child cut out the pictures and glue the ones that rhyme with *snow* onto the snowflakes.

Then help little ones work on number words with the reproducible on page 14. To complete the page, a child reads the number word on each snowman's broom, then writes the corresponding numeral on the the snowman's hat and draws a corresponding set of buttons on his tummy.

9

Snowflake Pattern
Use with "It's 'Snow' Much Fun To Read!" on page 9.

(title)

(title)

(title)

(student's name)

thinks it's
"snow" much fun
to READ!

(title)

(title)

(title)

Shapely Snowflakes

Match blocks.
Color shapes.
Design a new snowflake.

Does It Rhyme With *Snow?* Yes Or No?

Glue the pictures that rhyme with *snow* to the snowflakes.

√ Name _____

Frosty Friends

Read each word.
Write the numeral on the hat.
Draw a set of buttons to match.

three

two

four

eight

nine

five

six

one

MARVELOUS MITTENS

Youngsters will warm right up to these
mitten ideas for language and math!

Mitten Booklet

Count on this adorable booklet to help students practice math, language, *and* fine-motor skills. For each child, make five copies of page 17 and one copy of page 18. To make a booklet, a child follows these steps:

1. Cut out the text boxes and glue them in place, putting the odd numbers on the left side of each page and the even numbers on the right, as shown.
2. Write the corresponding numeral in the space below each mitten.
3. Color the mittens as desired.
4. Cut out the booklet pages along the bold lines; then glue the pages together end-to-end as indicated. Cut off the overlap area on page 10.
5. Lay a 46-inch length of yarn across the top of the connected pages so that the yarn touches each mitten cuff like a clothesline. Glue the yarn in place.
6. Add a small colored paper clip "clothespin" at the top of each page.
7. Fold the booklet accordion-style.
8. Make a cover illustration by tracing around one hand—fingers together—on construction paper. Cut out the resulting mitten shape and glue it to the booklet cover (the back side of page 1).
9. Write the title "10 Mittens" and your name on the cover.

For more elaborate illustrations, read through the suggestions below and gather the necessary materials. Then invite youngsters to illustrate their booklets using these options.

- Use watercolor markers to color horizontal stripes on a mitten.
- Draw and color your first initial on a mitten; then color the rest of the mitten a different color.
- Glue on a construction-paper mitten shape; then decorate it with glitter glue.
- Use crayons to color a pattern on a mitten.
- Paint a mitten with tempera paint; then add white paper-punch dots.
- Lay the page on top of corrugated cardboard; then make a crayon rubbing over a mitten.
- Glue on a fabric mitten shape.
- Use a crayon to draw and color vertical stripes on a mitten.
- Sponge-paint a mitten with tempera paint; then glue on rickrack stripes.
- Glue on a patterned-gift-wrap mitten shape.

A Clothesline Alphabet

While the mittens are hanging out to dry, why not have a little alphabet practice? Duplicate a copy of page 19 for each child. Have him fill in the missing letters to complete the alphabet. Refer youngsters to your classroom alphabet display if they need help.

A Mitten Melody

Cozy up to some more counting practice with this mathematic melody about mittens. After singing the song through once, encourage your students to suggest other descriptive words to replace the word *fuzzy,* such as *cozy, snuggly,* or *woolly.* If desired, create a set of ten felt mitten shapes and invite youngsters to sing the song and use the felt mittens at your flannelboard during center time.

Ten Fuzzy Mittens

One fuzzy, two fuzzy, three fuzzy mittens,
Four fuzzy, five fuzzy, six fuzzy mittens,
Seven fuzzy, eight fuzzy, nine fuzzy mittens,
Ten fuzzy mittens for wintertime!

Mitten Math

Mittens make marvelous manipulatives! Use real mittens or mitten shapes cut from wallpaper samples and invite youngsters to sort, pattern, and count them. Follow up with the reproducible on page 20. Have each child count and then graph the mittens of each design.

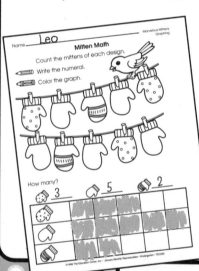

Get Your Mitts On These Books!

The Mitten
Written & Illustrated by Jan Brett
Published by The Putnam Publishing Group

Runaway Mittens
Written by Jean Rogers
Published by Greenwillow Books

The Mitten Tree
Written by Candace Christiansen
Published by Fulcrum Kids

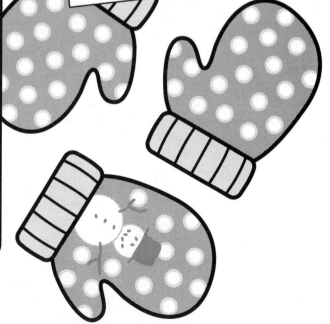

Overlap and glue here.

Overlap and glue here.

One mitten I see.

Two mittens for me.

Three mittens to show.

Four mittens for snow.

Five mittens are warm.

Six mittens for a storm.

Seven mittens are nice.

Eight mittens for ice.

Nine mittens for cold weather.

Ten mittens altogether!

Name

Letters On The Line

Say the alphabet.
Write the missing letters.

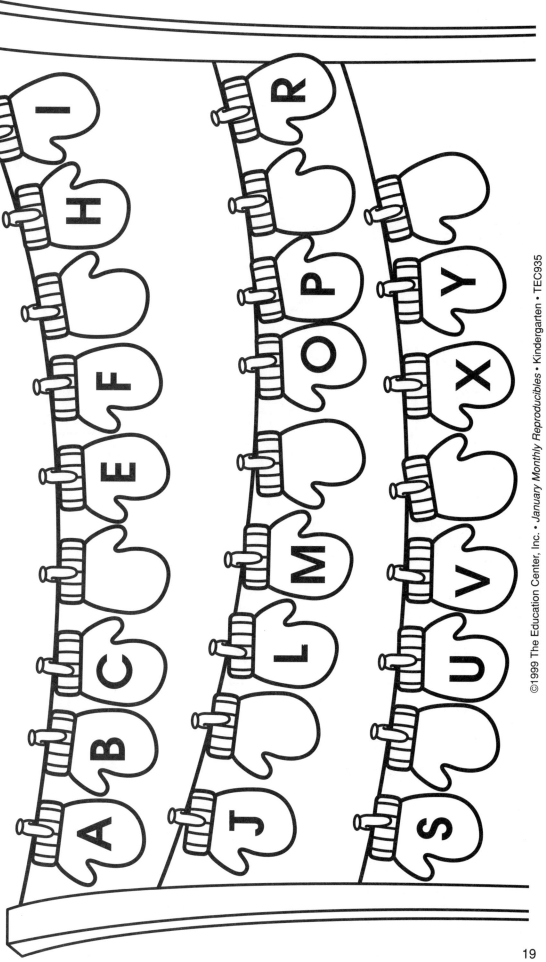

Mitten Math

Count the mittens of each design.

Write the numeral.

Color the graph.

How many?

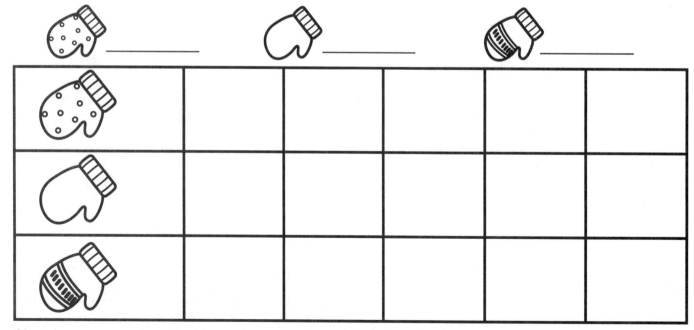

Breakfast Bonanza

Eggs, cereal, juice, pancakes…the breakfast choices go on and on. And so do the useful reproducible ideas in this unit! Enjoy!

Rise 'n' Shine!

Up and at 'em for some sequencing practice! Give each child a copy of page 23 and a sentence strip . Invite him to color the pictures and cut them apart. Direct him to glue the pictures to the sentence strip to reflect the sequence he follows each morning. When everyone has finished, invite youngsters to share and compare their morning routines. Who eats breakfast at home? Who eats breakfast at school? Who gets dressed after eating breakfast? Who gets dressed before? Be sure to tell students where breakfast falls in *your* morning routine, too.

Breakfast Booklet

What are your youngsters' favorite sights and sounds at breakfast? Find out when they complete these minibooklets. Begin by discussing breakfast and focusing youngsters' attention on their senses. Draw a simple chart on your chalkboard or a sheet of chart paper labeled with the headings "Sights," "Sounds," Tastes," "Textures," and "Smells." Ask youngsters to fill in the chart with breakfast-related words or phrases. Then duplicate a copy of page 24 for each child. Have each child color the booklet cover and draw an illustration for each page. Then have her cut out the cover and pages, stack them in order, and staple them along the left side. Send the minibooklets home for youngsters to share with their families.

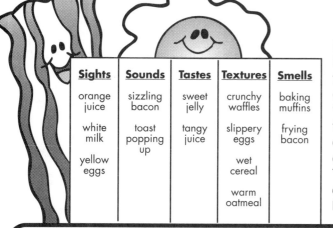

Sights	Sounds	Tastes	Textures	Smells
orange juice	sizzling bacon	sweet jelly	crunchy waffles	baking muffins
white milk	toast popping up	tangy juice	slippery eggs	frying bacon
yellow eggs			wet cereal	
			warm oatmeal	

How Do You Like Your Porridge?

Bring a bit of science and health into your breakfast unit. Read aloud the nursery rhyme "Pease Porridge Hot." Then prepare a few servings of instant oatmeal. Give each child a taste of the oatmeal while it is warm; then refrigerate the rest. Later, give each student a taste of the cold oatmeal. Which did your students prefer?

Save the remaining oatmeal (in a covered container) in your classroom for a few days. Have students examine the leftover oatmeal after a few days. How does it look? How does it smell? Stress the importance of storing food properly and discuss why we refrigerate foods. Some like it hot, some like it cold, but don't ever eat it if it's nine days old!

Pease porridge hot;
Pease porridge cold;
Pease porridge in the pot
Nine days old.

Red, Yellow, Blue— Breakfast For You!

Bring in a box of multicolored cereal (such as Froot Loops® cereal) for a little practice with both sorting and color words. Give each child a handful of cereal and a sheet of white paper. Ask her to sort the cereal by color and then glue the sorted pieces to the paper. Then have her write or copy the color word on the paper below each group. Follow up by having students complete the reproducible on page 25.

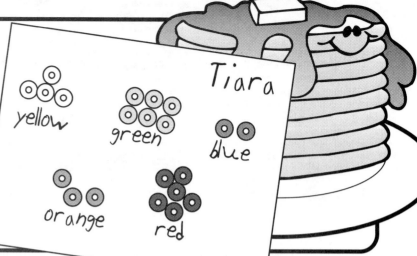

A Skill-Packed Placemat

This placemat project will help little ones practice fine-motor control, visual discrimination, and skip counting. And they'll love using it every day with their morning meals! To prepare, duplicate a class supply of pages 26, 27, and 28. You'll also need crayons and a class supply of 12" x 18" construction paper (in various colors). Begin by showing children *The Cheerios® Play Book* by Lee Wade (Little Simon). In this bright board book, youngsters use real Cheerios® cereal to complete the illustrations. Once they're familiar with the book, tell youngsters they're going to make a placemat they can use in the same way.

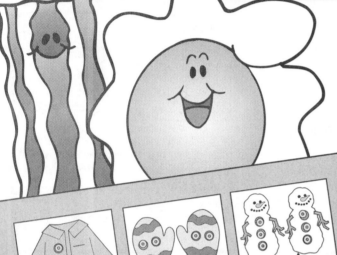

Have each child color the pictures on her copies of pages 26, 27, and 28. Have her find the circles in each picture and write the corresponding numeral on the line. Then have her cut out the pictures on the bold lines and arrange them as shown on a large sheet of construction paper. Have her glue the pictures in place. Then laminate all the placemats. Hand out Cheerios® cereal (or any small, round cereal) and invite students to place the cereal pieces on top of the circles in each picture, counting as they go. Send the placemats home so youngsters can use them at breakfast each day.

A Breakfast Song

Use a new version of a favorite silly song to promote phonemic awareness and get your little ones singing about the most important meal of the day!

Apple Jacks® And Waffles
(sung to the tune of "Apples And Bananas")

I like to eat, eat, eat
Apple Jacks® and waffles.
I like to eat, eat, eat
Apple Jacks® and waffles.

Repeat five times, each time substituting a different long vowel sound for the long e sound in "eat" and for the short a sound in "Apple Jacks®" and in "waffles."

Breakfast
Is
"Sense-ational"!

by _____

©1999 The Education Center, Inc.

My favorite sight at breakfast:

1

My favorite sound at breakfast:

2

My favorite smell at breakfast:

3

My favorite texture at breakfast:

4

My favorite taste at breakfast:

5

Red, Yellow, Blue—Breakfast For You!

Read and [crayon] color.

orange

blue

yellow

orange

green

red

yellow

blue

green

red

Placemat Patterns

Use with "A Skill-Packed Placemat" on page 22.

How many? _____

How many? _____

How many? _____

How many? _____

Placemat Patterns

Use with "A Skill-Packed Placemat" on page 22.

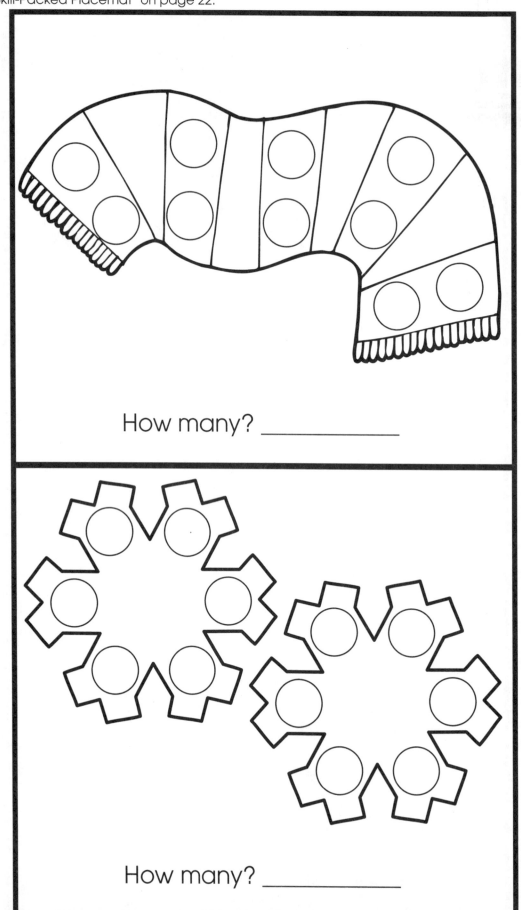

How many? _____

How many? _____

The third Monday in January is set aside as a day to honor Dr. Martin Luther King, Jr., a civil rights leader who dreamed of peace and love. Share his important message with your kindergartners.

A Dream Mobile ✓

Give your students some background information on Martin Luther King, Jr., by reading an appropriate picture book about him, such as *Happy Birthday, Martin Luther King* by Jean Marzollo (Scholastic Inc.). Tell youngsters about King's famous "I Have A Dream" speech and explain that King touched many people with his wish for peace and love among all people. Then invite them to make a mobile representing King's message.

For each child, duplicate the patterns on pages 30 and 31 onto white construction paper. To make a mobile, a child follows these steps:

1. Cut out the cloud shapes and punch holes as indicated.
2. Write the date for Martin Luther King, Jr. Day on the line.
3. With the holes at the bottom, glue the clouds end-to-end to form a circle.
4. Color the star, heart, and dove patterns; then cut them out and punch holes as indicated.
5. Glue some silver glitter onto the star.
6. Glue some red tissue-paper squares onto the heart.
7. Glue some white craft feathers onto the dove.

When all the pieces are ready, attach them to the cloud circle with lengths of string or yarn. Punch two opposite holes at the top of the cloud circle and add a string or yarn hanger as shown. Display the finished mobiles hanging from your classroom ceiling. Hope, love, and peace—now those are things to look up to!

The Content Of Our Character

Dr. King said that he hoped one day his children would be judged by the content of their character. Discuss what this means with your students. What qualities does each child possess that make her a special person? Make a list similar to the one shown, and discuss examples of when your students may have exhibited each character trait. Then encourage each child to make a poster to tell about her character. Give each child a copy of page 32. Invite each youngster to color the figure to look like herself. Then have her choose one of the traits from your discussion. In the space provided, write her dictation as she describes a time when she displayed that character trait. Display the posters on a bulletin board with the title "These Kids Have Character!"

Mobile Patterns

Use with "A Dream Mobile" on page 29.

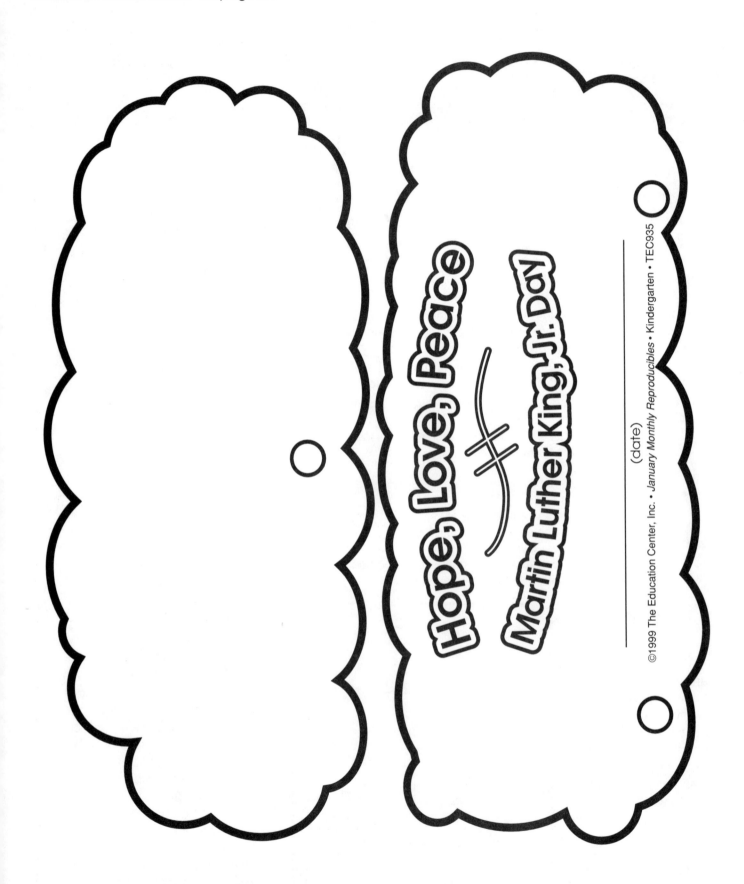

Hope, Love, Peace

Martin Luther King, Jr. Day

_____ (date)

Name _____

Dr. King had a dream,
A wish, a hope, a plea,
That I'd be judged for who I am:
A very special me!

I show _____ when I...
(character trait)

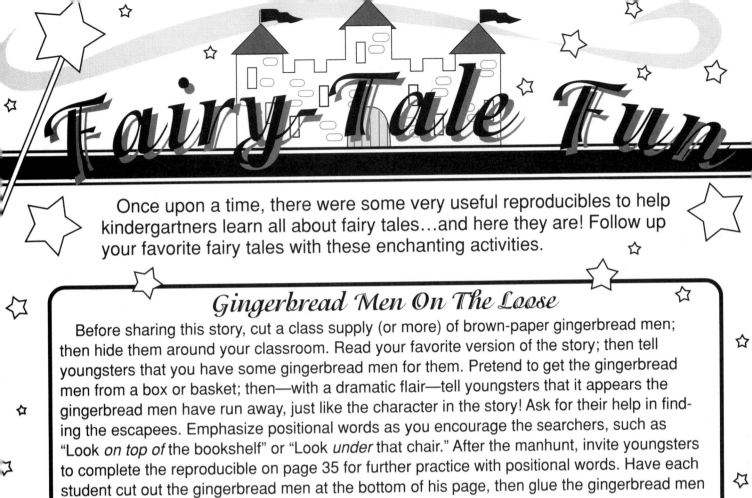

Fairy-Tale Fun

Once upon a time, there were some very useful reproducibles to help kindergartners learn all about fairy tales…and here they are! Follow up your favorite fairy tales with these enchanting activities.

Gingerbread Men On The Loose

Before sharing this story, cut a class supply (or more) of brown-paper gingerbread men; then hide them around your classroom. Read your favorite version of the story; then tell youngsters that you have some gingerbread men for them. Pretend to get the gingerbread men from a box or basket; then—with a dramatic flair—tell youngsters that it appears the gingerbread men have run away, just like the character in the story! Ask for their help in finding the escapees. Emphasize positional words as you encourage the searchers, such as "Look *on top of* the bookshelf" or "Look *under* that chair." After the manhunt, invite youngsters to complete the reproducible on page 35 for further practice with positional words. Have each student cut out the gingerbread men at the bottom of his page, then glue the gingerbread men in place on the picture, following the directions below.

— Put one gingerbread man *at the top of* the stairs.
— Put one gingerbread man *in the middle of* the rug.
— Put one gingerbread man *behind* the sofa.
— Put one gingerbread man *above* the window.
— Put one gingerbread man *on top of* the table.
— Put one gingerbread man *in front of* the door.
— Put one gingerbread man *between* the sofa and the table.
— Put one gingerbread man *below* the picture.

A Huff-And-Puff Prop

Enhance a telling of *The Three Little Pigs* with this fun prop. To make one, duplicate the wolf pattern on page 36 onto tagboard. Color it and cut out the mouth as indicated, adjusting the size of the circle to fit the end of a handheld hair dryer. Plug in the hair dryer and have it ready in your group area. Then read or tell the story of *The Three Little Pigs.* Each time the Big Bad Wolf huffs and puffs, turn on the dryer (cool setting) and direct it at your little piggies. It'll blow them away!

Extend the learning later with a small-group experiment. On a table, place several objects, such as a crayon, a book, a block, and a cotton ball. Ask students to predict whether the air blown from the dryer will move each object; then direct the dryer at each one and discuss the results.

This Is The Way To Grandma's House

Review numerical order for the numbers 1–30 with the maze on page 37. Tell your students to help Little Red Riding Hood find the way to Grandma's house. Watch out for wolves!

Does The Little Red Hen Do That?

After sharing your favorite version of *The Little Red Hen,* have your little ones recall the events in the story. Give each child a copy of page 38. Instruct her to cut out all the pictures at the bottom of the page, then choose only those pictures that show tasks the Little Red Hen performs in the story. Have her glue those pictures in sequence in the boxes. As an extension, have each student use one of the remaining pictures as inspiration for a new story about the hardworking Little Red Hen. Have the student glue that picture on the back of her paper and write, dictate, or draw her story there.

If I Met A Troll

What would your youngsters do if they came face-to-face with a troll like the one in *The Three Billy Goats Gruff?* Invite them to tell you all about it! Duplicate the story starter on page 39 for each child. Encourage him to cut out his pattern, then write and illustrate his story in the open space. Have each child color the troll peekover, or provide craft materials—such as wiggle eyes, yarn, or pipe cleaner pieces—for youngsters to use in adding creative touches to their trolls. Display the peekover stories on a bulletin board with the title "Troll Tales."

If I met a troll...

I would give him a cookie and ask him to be my friend. He probably is just lonely, and that's why he's so grumpy.

Rosalita

Fairy-Tale Lotto

Here's a fun wrap-up for your fairy-tale unit that will have youngsters practicing their listening and matching skills. Duplicate a class supply plus one extra of the lotto board on page 40. Cut one board into 16 squares to use as caller cards. Trim the remaining boards along the bold outside lines; then make four different versions of the gameboard by cutting each one so that it has only nine squares, as shown.

Before playing, show the students all 16 caller cards and identify the fairy tale illustrated on each one. Then give each child a gameboard and nine markers, such as pennies or plastic chips. Call out one fairy tale at a time and show the card, if desired. If a child has the matching illustration on her card, she may cover it with a game marker. Continue until one child covers three boxes in a row (or, if desired, her whole card) and yells out, "Happily Ever After!" Then invite youngsters to switch gameboards and play again. The end!

Name _____

Over Here, Under There—Gingerbread Men Everywhere!

Listen. ✂ Cut. 🧴 Glue.

35

Wolf Pattern
Use with "A Huff-And-Puff Prop" on page 33.

Name _____

On The Way To Grandma's House

Count.
Trace the path to help Little Red Riding Hood find Grandma's house.

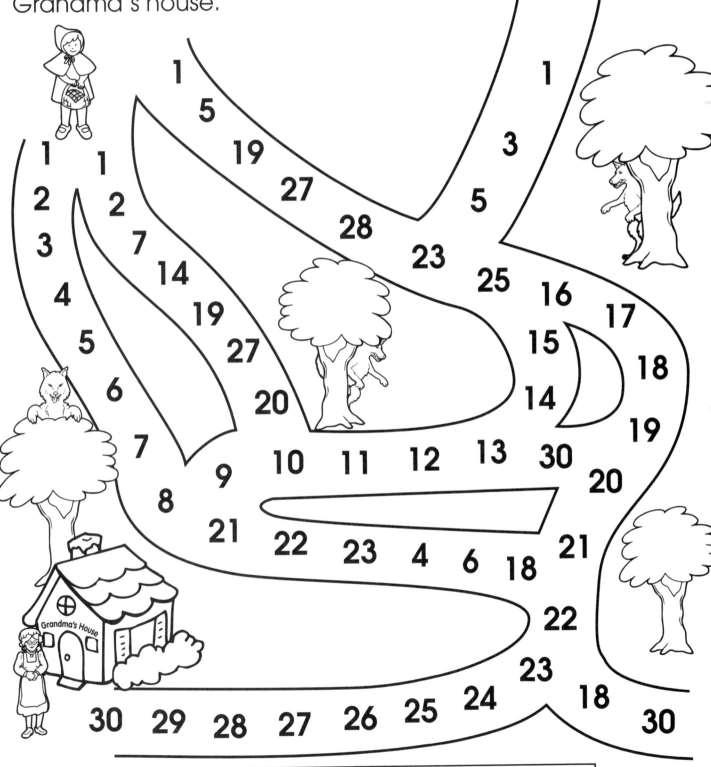

Bonus Box: Write the numerals 1–30 on the back of your paper.

A Hardworking Hen

What does the Little Red Hen do?

 Cut.

Glue.

1	**2**	**3**

Bonus Box: Use a leftover picture to make up a new story about the Little Red Hen. Draw it on the back of your paper.

If I met   a troll...

Fairy-Tale Lotto Board

Use with "Fairy-Tale Lotto" on page 34.

POLAR BEARS

They're big. They're white. And they're on these pages, just perfect for helping little ones learn math, science, and more!

More Fish? Or Fewer?

Although a polar bear's favorite meal is seal, it also likes to eat fish. So let some fishing polar bears help your youngsters practice comparing sets with the math mat on page 42. For small-group use, duplicate a few copies of the mat and laminate them for durability. Give each student in a small group a mat and a supply of Goldfish® crackers. Together, count the fish in the first picture; then have each child in the group make a larger set (in the open space next to the ice) using his fish crackers. Discuss the various answers. Continue making sets of more or fewer fish as directed for each box.

For whole-group practice, duplicate the page for each child. Have each student draw sets of more or fewer fish in each box as indicated.

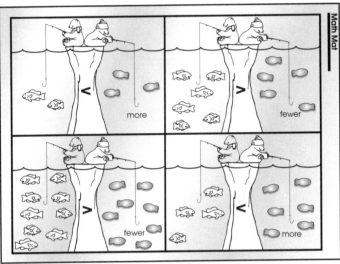

Math Mat

Palatable Polar Bears

Serve up a polar bear–inspired treat at snacktime. Duplicate page 44 for each child and provide the ingredients for students to make the polar bear cookies pictured. Encourage each child to follow the steps to create her own "un-bear-ably" delicious snack!

Chillin' Out

Polar bears love the snowy, icy weather of the Arctic region. Their thick fur and sharp claws make them well adapted to life on the ice. Use the polar bear's affinity for chilly temperatures to review the concepts of cold and hot. Explain that you are going to name several items, one at a time. If the item named is cold, students should respond, "Polar bear!" If the item named is hot, they should remain silent. Here's a list to get you started:

the inside of a refrigerator
a candle's flame
a milkshake
a snowflake
an iceberg
a volcano
the sun

Follow up with the reproducible on page 43. Have each student color the pictures at the bottom of her page and then cut them apart. Direct her to glue the pictures that show cold items onto the snowflakes.

41

Math Mat

Use with "More Fish? Or Fewer?" on page 41.

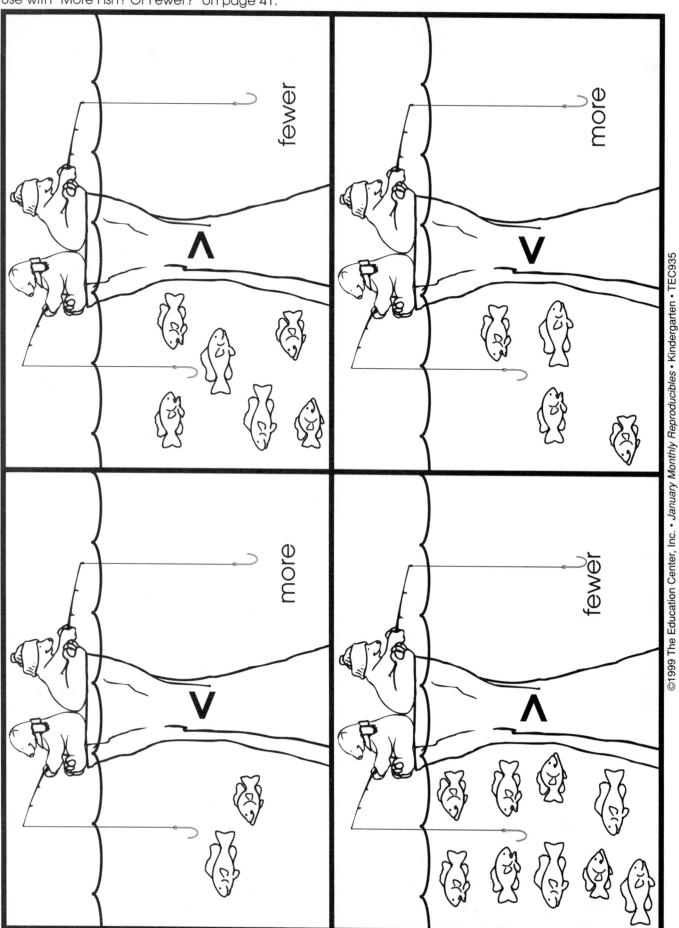

Polar Bears Like The Cold!

Color.　　　　Cut.

43

Polar Bear Fare

You will need:

 1 Oreo® cookie

 2 raisins

 white frosting

 1 dark brown M&M's® candy

 2 minimarshmallows

 **1** Spread white frosting on the Oreo® cookie.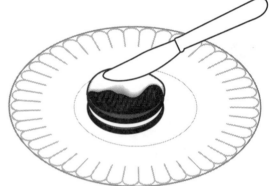

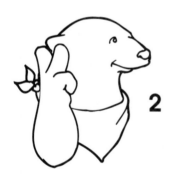 **2** Add minimarshmallow ears.

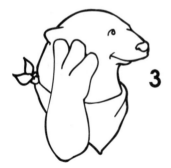 **3** Make a face with the raisins and the M&M's® candy.

Calendar Concepts

Make a date to reinforce calendar skills with the helpful ideas in this unit!

Mark Your Calendar

Help your students improve their calendar skills by marking upcoming events on your classroom calendar. Duplicate a supply of the calendar markers on page 46. Color the markers as desired; then cut them apart. At the beginning of each month, attach markers to your calendar to note weekly happenings, such as art class or a trip to the computer lab, and to note special events, such as birthdays, visitors, or days off. Each day when you review the calendar with your class, point out the marked days and ask questions like "How many days until our field trip?" or "What's happening on the third Tuesday of this month?" Before you know it, your youngsters will be calendar experts!

S	M	T	W
1	2	3	Field Trip
		10	11

FEBRU

Chicken Soup All Year

Warm up your storytime with the delightful poetry of Maurice Sendak's *Chicken Soup With Rice* (Scholastic Inc.). Afterward, make a class book that focuses on the months of the year. First make a chart listing all the months. Discuss each month, noting the typical weather or holidays that occur at that time of year. Then give each child a white construction-paper copy of page 47. Invite each student to cut out the pattern along the bold lines, then fold the soup-bowl shape up as indicated. Encourage him to personalize the soup bowl and to write on the line his favorite month for eating chicken soup with rice. Fold the soup bowl back down; then write his dictated completion of the sentence behind the bowl shape. Then have him complete his page by drawing an illustration in the open space. Stack all the book pages together, add a construction-paper cover cut to match, and bind the book with metal rings along the top edge.

A Calendar Crown

Reward your students for conquering calendar skills with the awards on page 48. Duplicate a class supply of the page. Invite each child to color an award as she demonstrates each skill. When a child has earned all three awards, invite her to cut them out and glue them onto a sentence strip. Next, have her color and cut out the appropriate crown-topper pattern (king or queen), and then glue it to a tagboard semicircle. Complete the crown by stapling the semicircle to the sentence strip as shown and stapling the strip to fit the child's head. Your classroom will soon be full of calendar kings and queens!

Calendar Markers

Use with "Mark Your Calendar" on page 45.

Art	Art	Music	Music	Field Trip
PE	PE	Computer	Computer	Special Guest
Library	Library	Birthday	Birthday	Report Cards
Special Event	Special Event	Special Event	Show-And-Tell	Show-And-Tell
NO SCHOOL	NO SCHOOL	NO SCHOOL	NO SCHOOL	NO SCHOOL

I like chicken soup with rice

in _____ because...

(month)

Fold here.

I know the days of the week!

I know the months of the year!

I can count to 30!

Calendar Queen

Calendar King

Delightful Dinosaurs

Make no bones about it—your little ones will dig these dinosaur activities!

Crack Open A Surprise

Here's an "egg-citing" way to introduce your dinosaur unit! Duplicate a class supply of the patterns on pages 51 and 52 onto white copy paper, plus one extra set onto white construction paper. Color and decorate the construction-paper copies as desired; then cut out both patterns on the bold lines. Also cut along the zigzag line on the egg pattern. Then staple the two halves of the egg over the dinosaur pattern at the top and bottom. At circle time, show the paper egg to your students and read the poem aloud. After youngsters have had a chance to guess, reveal the dinosaur and tell them that dinosaurs will be the focus of your new unit.

Then give each child her own copies of the dinosaur and egg patterns, and invite her to make her own dinosaur surprise to share with her family.

Dinosaur Ditties

Stomp on over to the cassette player and pop in a tape of one of these tunes. They're "dino-mite"!

"If I Had A Dinosaur"
More Singable Songs For The Very Young
Sung by Raffi
Troubadour Records Ltd.

"Dicky, Dicky Dinosaur"
Diamonds And Dragons
Sung by Charlotte Diamond
Hug Bug Records

"The Day The Dinosaurs Came To School" and "In The Swamp Womp Womp"
Dinosaur Ride
Sung by Jim Valley And Friends
Rainbow Planet Records And Tapes

There is something in this egg that lived long ago.

Can you guess? Do you know?

Crack it open if you dare;
What you'll find is a "dino-mite" scare!

ROAR!

All About Dinosaurs

Your young scientists will be roaring about research when they complete the reproducible on page 53. Ask each child to choose a dinosaur of interest to him and to find out some simple facts about that dinosaur. (You may want to provide time and guidance on fact finding at school or do this as a parent-involvement project.) Give each child a copy of page 53 to color and complete. Then set aside a special time for your researchers to share what they've found out. Display the reports on a bulletin board with the title "Nobody Knows Dinosaurs Like [Teacher's Name]'s Class!"

Name _Casey_

My Dinosaur Report

Delightful Dinosaur Research

This dinosaur's name is _stegosaurus_
It measured _20 feet long_

It was a (plant eater) meat eater (Circle one.)
It walked on 2 legs (4 legs) (Circle one.)

Its special features include _plates on its back_ _a tiny brain_

Here is a picture of this dinosaur:

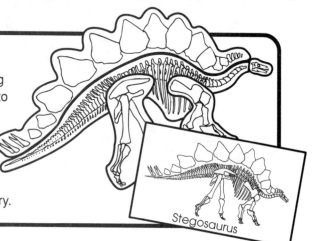
Stegosaurus

Skeleton Scatter

Give your little ones a chance to role-play paleontologists during center time. Duplicate the skeleton pieces on pages 54 and 55 onto tagboard. Cut the pieces out along the bold lines. Also cut out the boxes showing the assembled skeletons. Laminate the skeleton pieces; then bury them in your sand table. Invite each child who visits the sand table during center time to hunt for and assemble the two skeletons on a nearby tabletop. Have him use the pictures of the assembled skeletons as a guide if necessary.

That's A Whole Lotta Letters!

The lengthy names of dinosaurs make for plenty of letter-matching practice in this writing-center activity. To prepare, gather a supply of white paper, crayons, some ink pads, and a set of alphabet rubber stamps. Print the names of several dinosaurs on sentence strips. (Use either uppercase or lowercase letters, to match your alphabet stamps.) Add a sticker or small picture of the dinosaur to each strip. Invite each child who visits this center to choose a dinosaur name and stamp it on a sheet of paper, matching each printed letter with the corresponding rubber stamp. Then have him draw a story about his chosen dinosaur.

DIPLODOCUS

Build-A-Dino

Wrap up your dinosaur unit with this fun review. Duplicate a small-group supply of page 56 onto colorful construction paper. Cut apart the dinosaurs; then laminate the pieces, if desired. Place each set of pieces into a separate plastic bag. Use these dinosaur puzzles to play a game in which each child attempts to build a complete dinosaur. Give each child in a small group a set of puzzle pieces. Ask each child, in turn, a question about information learned during your dinosaur unit. For each correct answer, a child may put down a piece of her dinosaur. The first child to build her whole dinosaur wins the game.

As a variation, use the game to review basic concepts. On index cards, print letters, numerals, or sight words. Show a card to each child on her turn and—if she identifies it correctly—she may add a piece to her dinosaur puzzle. These prehistoric puzzles will be a favorite with your dino experts!

There is something in this egg that lived long ago.

Can you guess? Do you know?

Crack it open if you dare;

What you'll find is a "dino-mite" scare!

Dinosaur Pattern
Use with "Crack Open A Surprise" on page 49.

Name _____

 **My Dinosaur Report**

This dinosaur's name is _____.

It measured _____.

It was a   plant eater   meat eater   (Circle one.)

It walked on   2 legs   4 legs   (Circle one.)

Its special features include

_____

_____

Here is a picture of this dinosaur:

Dinosaur Skeleton Pieces

Use with "Skeleton Scatter" on page 50.

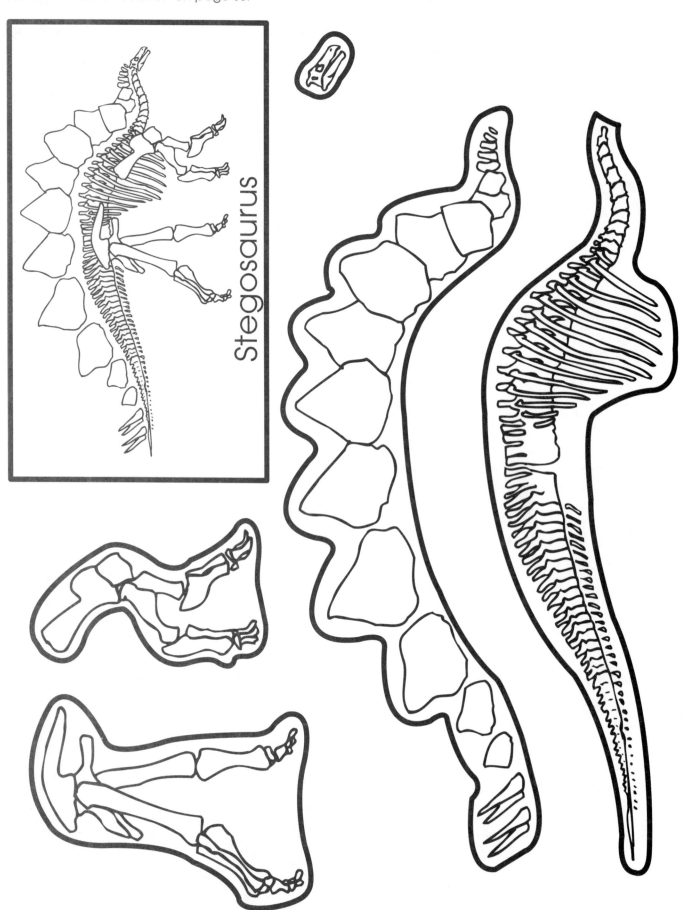

Stegosaurus

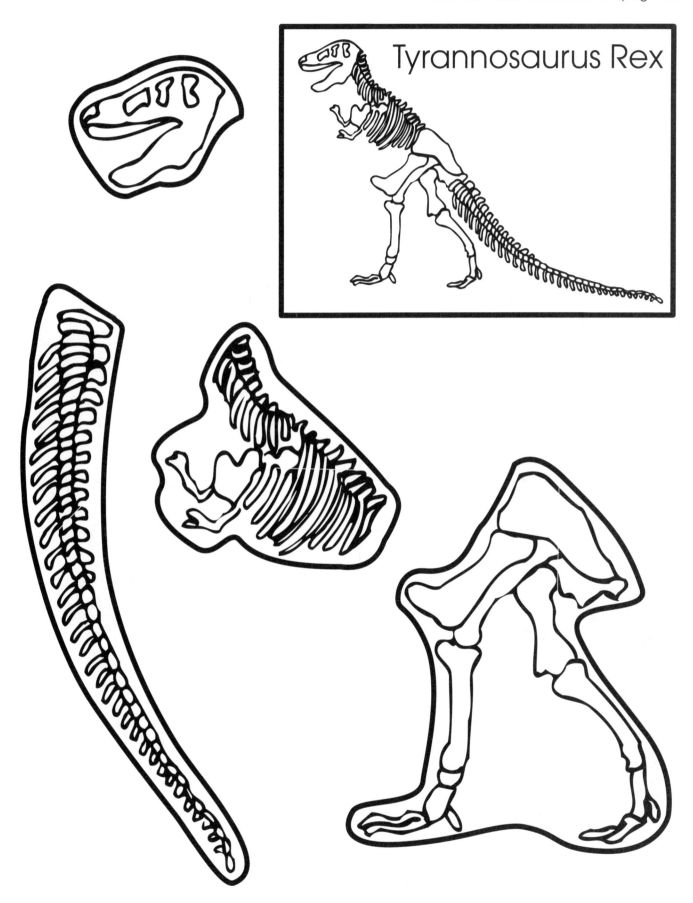

Tyrannosaurus Rex

Dinosaur Puzzle

Use with "Build-A-Dino" on page 50.

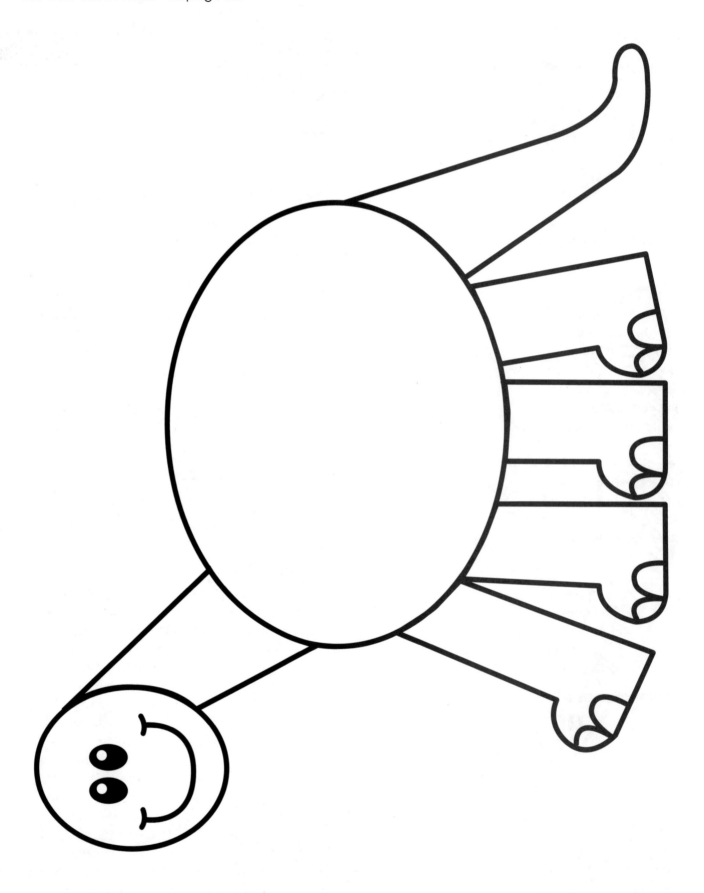

COMMUNITY HELPERS ON THE JOB

From astronauts to zookeepers, helpers make a community *work!*
Explore careers with the activities in this unit.

Check Your Yellow Pages

Where can you find community helpers? Just check the yellow pages of your local phone book! Bring in a phone book and show youngsters the yellow pages. Point out the various categories and show students the advertisements and listings. Can they guess some of the services just by looking at the pictures on some pages? Explain how adults use the yellow pages—to find workers who can provide services they need or stores that carry merchandise they want.

Then invite youngsters to create their own version of the yellow pages. Duplicate a class supply of page 59 on white paper and a class supply of page 60 on yellow paper. Ask one of your budding readers to describe a picture on her copy of page 59. Help her read the caption aloud. Then ask students to find the worker on their "yellow pages" (their copies of page 60) who can provide the needed service. Have each child cut out the box showing that worker and glue it along the top edge of the corresponding box on the white page where indicated. Continue until you've matched every worker to a need.

A Growing Community

Prepare this bulletin board to take note of the many workers who make up your community. First cover the board with light blue paper. Add the title and some clouds, as shown. Ask the children to help you choose several community destinations. Decorate different-colored sheets of construction paper to resemble those places; then mount them on the board so that they resemble a row of one-story buildings. Then cut a few corresponding sheets of construction paper into strips. Have each child choose a strip of paper to coordinate with one community place. Have him name a helper who works at that place. Label the strip with the helper; then mount it on the board to make the building "grow." Continue to add to the buildings on the display as children think of or learn about other helpers who work in each place.

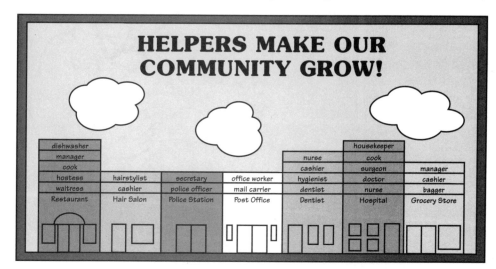

Community Helpers Flip Book

From top to bottom, your little ones will love this flip book! To prepare, duplicate a class supply of pages 61–64. Before handing out copies, discuss the clothing worn by various community helpers, as well as the tools helpers use. Then give each child a set of pages and tell students that they'll have to look carefully at these pictures of community helpers to match up the pages for their flip books.

To make a flip book, a child cuts out all his booklet pages along the bold lines. He carefully cuts along the dotted lines where indicated, stopping before the left margins. He stacks the cut pages in random order, then places the blank page at the bottom of the stack and the cover on top. He then staples the booklet along the left margin.

Once the flip books are assembled, challenge your students' listening skills. Ask them to listen to a clue, flip the pages to find the community helper described, and then color the page accordingly. After they've completed the directions below, invite students to color the rest of their booklets as they choose.

— I deliver the mail. Color my hat blue.
— I prepare food for people to eat. Color my scarf green.
— I help people stay healthy. Color my shirt pink.
— I help put out fires. Color my helmet red.
— I teach children at school. Color my hair bow purple.
— I repair broken appliances. Color my toolbox brown.
— What do you want to be when you grow up? Draw a picture of your career choice on the last page.

All Around The Town

This musical activity will give each child a chance to share his *current* career choice. To prepare, draw some simple lines on a paper plate to make it resemble a steering wheel. Then seat your students in a circle. Give the steering wheel to one child and invite him to "drive" all around the circle as everyone sings the tune below. When the third line is sung, have him stop in front of a seated child. At the end of the verse, that child stands up and announces her career choice. Then she takes the wheel and the former driver sits in her place. She then drives around as the song is repeated, stopping in front of someone else at the appropriate point in the song. Continue until every child has had a turn to drive.

All Around Our Town
(sung to the tune of "Pop Goes The Weasel")

All around our town you ride,
Looking for some helpers.
What does [child's name] want to be?
What kind of helper?

Name _____

Check Your Yellow Pages

Find a worker to help.
Glue.

I need a haircut.

Glue here.

I need to buy groceries.

Glue here.

I need some good books.

Glue here.

We need a day care center.

Glue here.

I need a pipe fixed.

Glue here.

I need to have trash hauled.

Glue here.

Yellow Page

Use with "Check Your Yellow Pages" on page 57.

Sanitation Worker

Librarian

Day Care Worker

Plumber

Hairdresser

Cashier

Me...when I grow up.

COMMUNITY
HELPERS
Flip Book

Name _____

©1999 The Education Center, Inc.

Flip Book Pages

Use with "Community Helpers Flip Book" on page 58.

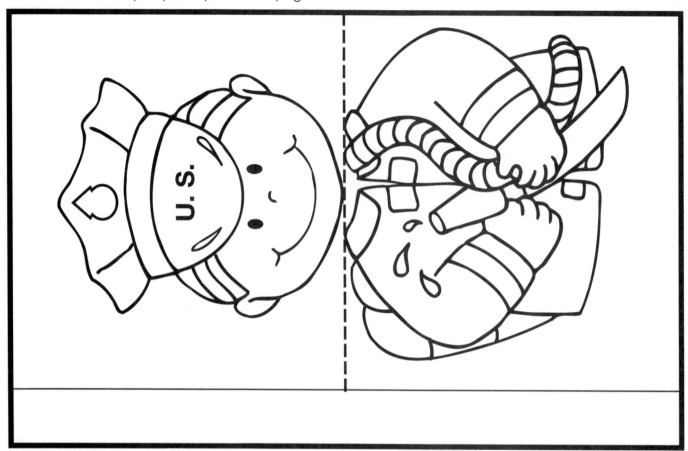

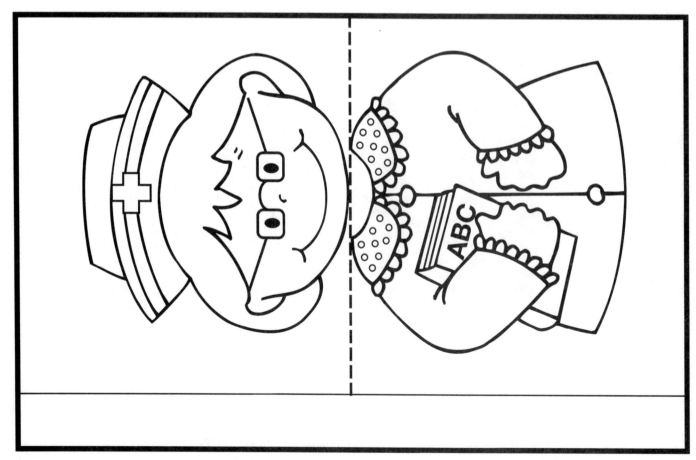

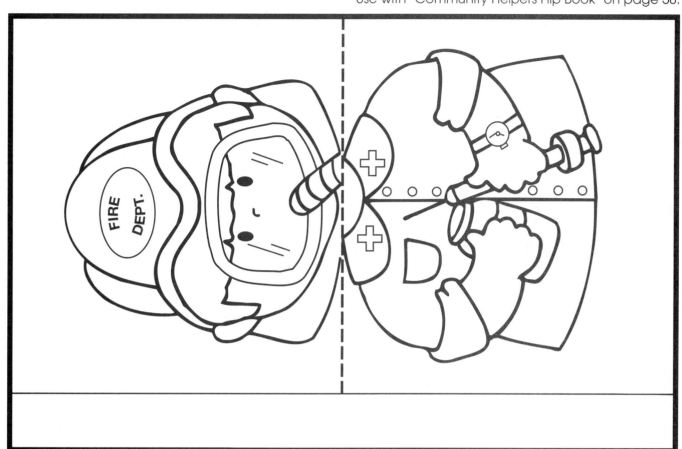

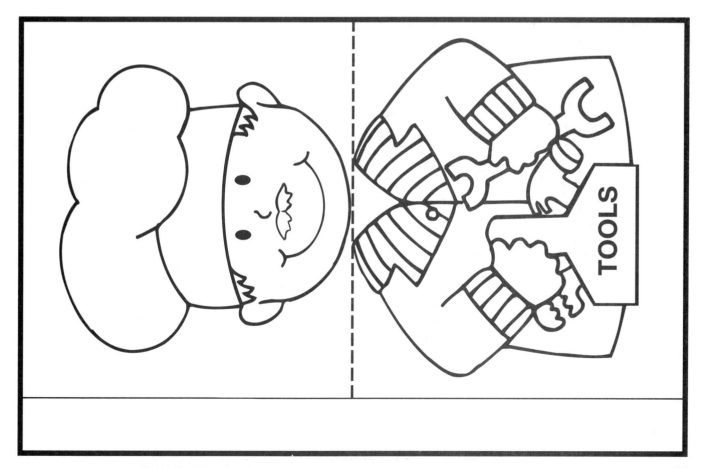

Flip Book Pages
Use with "Community Helpers Flip Book" on page 58.

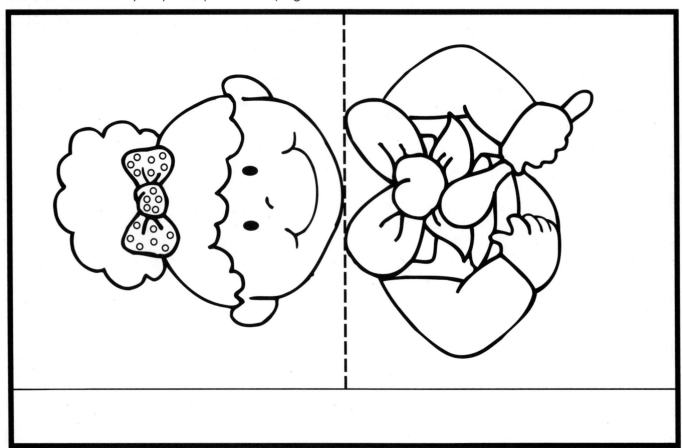

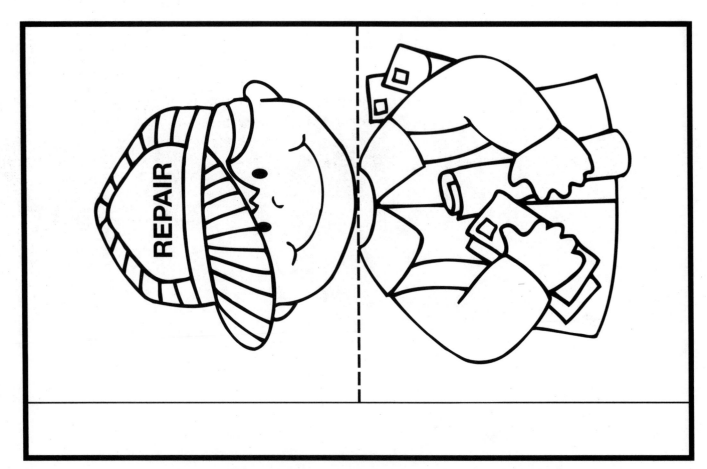